The Booya Guide to Great Public Speaking

How to Speak and Present Like the Pro's

Published by Martin Presse

Copyright 2011 Martin Presse

Printed in the United States of America

Presse, Martin
> The Booya Guide To Great Public Speaking,
> Learn to Speak and Present Like the Pros
> /Martin Presse. -- 1st ed.

ISBN: 978-0-9868094-0-8

Cover & Layout Design by: MicroArts Pvt Ltd
> http://microarts.biz

Photos by: Jasper's Studio - Wetaskiwin, Alberta, Canada

Warning - Disclaimer

Acknowledgements

There are so many people to thank and show appreciation for. I always tell people I won the lottery when it came to parenting. I lost my dad in 2009 but I'll never lose my love and devotion for him. My mom is still simply the best. My brothers and sister have been great friends and mentors. I may not be near you very often but you are always in my thoughts. Craig Valentine, my coach, mentor and friend. The first professional speaker to say, "Martin, you can do this for a living. I really think you can." I'll never forget standing on your front porch the last day I took one-on-one training with you. You shared some words with me that day that absolutely changed my life. You get a free copy of the book my friend. I only recently met Craig Duswalt but I suspect we'll be friends. Without his advice this book would have come out in 2013, would have been 330 pages, with a readership of eight. Special thanks to Nancy Brook, author and speaker, for showing me what it means to be persistent.

Many thanks to countless others: Lorrene Thiessen, Darren Lacroix, Carla Coates, Kitty Hevener, Toastmasters International, CMA Entertainment out of Winnipeg and Wayne Lee. All of you have played a special role in helping me develop as a speaker, entertainer and a person. To all my former managers, thank you for all the time off so I could do what I love. To the ladies in the office, the mauve shirt made all the difference.

Booya!

Dedication

To Patti, Kali and Alex

You have been the greatest gift any man could ask for. I cherish every
moment we have. Thank you for letting me be a part of your lives.
I will love you always.

Martin

About the Author

Martin Presse is an award winning keynote speaker from Alberta, Canada, right next to the majestic Rocky Mountains. It was while growing up in a bilingual community in southern Quebec that Martin developed a passion for speaking and entertainment. First came Elvis impersonations for family and eventually some acting lessons in Montreal while in University

In August 2008, Martin entered Toastmasters International World Championship of Public Speaking and finished in the top ten out of 30,000 contestants from around the world.

Martin hasn't stopped speaking since then. Today, Martin travels across North America presenting keynote speeches and performing comedy stage hypnosis shows. He also coaches individuals who want to improve their speaking skills.

Table of Contents

Introduction

The Booya Guide

In 2001 I was asked to emcee a small-town country music concert, no more than six acts. All I had to do was welcome everyone at the start of the evening and introduce the acts. "Oh, and Martin, don't forget to be funny."

No problem. Three-hundred-and-fifty people walked through the doors. As each person entered my heart beat just a little bit faster. You can imagine just how fast it was racing by the time the last person walked in. I was losing my mind with fear. My hands shook, I lost all control of my voice and breathing became a labor-intensive exercise. Five minutes before the event started I locked myself in a bathroom stall. My mind rebelled.

Martin you cannot do this.
These people will tear you apart.
Who do you think you are? You aren't an entertainer. You aren't a speaker.
What makes you think these people want to see you up there?
Tonight will be the worst night of your life.

Seconds before being introduced I made my way to the side of the stage. I knew with absolute certainty something terrible was about to happen. I was going to pee myself right then and there. The event organizer announced my name and I walked out onto the stage. Each step felt like a thousand miles. I couldn't hear a sound. My mind went blank. I was going to die.

I placed my hand around the microphone and said, "I really have to go to the bathroom, please welcome (some band)" and walked off stage to tremendous laughter and applause.

Wait a second, they were laughing. They thought I was being funny! I went to the bathroom and came back to the stage, this time with a totally different attitude. If I could tell them about my toilet needs and get a huge laugh then I could be myself and just have fun with them. A Booya Speaker was born.

What exactly is Booya and what is the Booya Guide to Great Public Speaking? Booya is an attitude. It's a way of living. It's about having passion, purpose and commitment.

Booya Speakers open big, tell a great story and close big. You'll read later on how opening big means something quite different than what you probably think it does. Everybody remembers the Booya Speaker. Everybody talks about the emotionally-charged toast, the un-forgettable speech, or the extraordinary keynote Booya Speakers make.

Booya Speakers never open a speech with: "Hi, I want to thank the organizing committee for inviting me here today. I am truly hon-ored..."

Booya Speakers wait for the applause to end, they stand con-fidently at center stage, look straight out into the audience and begin strong.

Here's an example: "I was told by no less than five high school teachers that I would never amount to anything. Raise your hand if you have ever been told something like that." That's a strong opening. It's memorable and gets the audience thinking within seconds of you utter-ing your first word.

The purpose of this book is to help anyone making a wedding toast, a sales presentation, a short five-minute speech at a business meeting, or a ninety-minute keynote. If your goal is to be more confident during any one of these situations this book will definitely help you get there. Public speaking is about having emotion, passion, purpose and commitment. The worst thing you can do as a speaker is to be boring so don't be afraid to show some attitude.

Booya!

Chapter 1

In The Beginning

One of the objectives of this book is to keep the process as simple as possible. My goal is to give you the most important information and make it understandable so you can apply it quickly and easily.

It won't come as a surprise that any speech or presentation should have a beginning, middle and an end. I am, however, going to show you valuable techniques that you can use in each of these sections. You might have heard other speakers tell you to use this method when giving a speech:

1)   Tell them what you're going to tell them
2)   Tell them
3)   Tell them what you told them

Do not follow this worn-out formula. That's what most audiences expect you to do. As a Booya Speaker you want to WOW them with the unexpected. Never be predictable. The greatest speakers in the world are unique in their delivery. That's what makes them fantastic. They come at you from every angle and you never see it coming.

We're going to start off with the technical parts of the speech. Just like an essay or article the speech itself is broken down into the introduction, the body and conclusion. The key is to break down each of the parts and deal with them separately. You want to breathe life into each of the parts and make them powerful on their own. When you bring them together, POW! You have one incredible speech.

Introduction

How many times have you heard someone start a speech with the boring "thank you's?" Don't fall into that trap. You don't have to do it. There is no rule that says you have to—somebody started doing it and somehow everyone else decided it was what you were supposed to do. It's NOT! It's the safe thing to do. It's the predictable thing to do and it's the least memorable thing you can do. The first ninety seconds of your speech will determine if the audience will pay attention to the rest of your speech. If you lose them in the first ninety seconds, you'll be facing an uphill battle trying to get them back.

Break out of the mold and get rid of the unnecessary thank you's. You want to capture your audience's attention right from the get go. There are much better options.

Option One – Get Right Into A Story

Capture your audience's attention by jumping into a story right away. It can start with something like these openings:

1) *I can clearly remember the first time I fell in love. I was 9 years old and her name was Nancy B. (I have to protect the innocent!)*

2) *I had no alternative other than to climb the nearest tree and ask God for some help.*

3) *Bully, as I liked to call him, came down the hallway and I was fully aware he was looking for nobody else but me. I knew, without a doubt, my life was about to end—or begin.*

Boom! You've got your audience hooked and paying attention

right away.

Booya!

Option Two – Ask A Question

Another way to capture your audience's attention is to get on stage, pause and ask a question. I guarantee you the audience is not expecting this. You will have immediately captured their attention AND engaged them. There is a caveat here, you want to ask a question that the majority of the audience will agree with. In other words you want their buy in. Getting them to agree with you also establishes trust and credibility right off the bat. Here are some examples:

"Raise your hand if you're even been in love."

"Raise your hand if you've ever been hurt."

"Raise your hand if you've ever had a time of financial difficulty."

Don't ask a question that could evoke twelve different opinions. For example:

"Raise your hand if you think Bill Clinton was the greatest President."

Some people may think he was but there are many different viable opinions as to who was the best President."

A better question regarding the Presidency might be:
"Raise your hand if you think the President should have tremendous leadership ability."

I'm willing to bet 99% of the audience will agree with you.

Once you've asked the question and gotten agreement, go right into your story. Here's an example:

> *"Raise your hand if you have ever been in love."*

Pause.

> *"Good, I'm glad to see most of you have."*

Pause.

> *"I can clearly remember the first time I laid eyes on Nancy B. I was nine years old and we were at the local swimming pool."*

Did you notice I never asked the question this way, "How many of you …?"

You should always speak to your audience as if they are one person. Craig Valentine, my speaking coach says, "Speak to one, look to many." The point is that you want everyone in the room to feel like you are talking directly to them. You can achieve this by asking a "you" focused question. "Have you …" "Will you …" or "When was the last time you…" Never ask "how many" because it doesn't really matter if it was two, twenty-two or the hundred twenty-two. You can, however, make it matter to one person by using "you."

Option Three – Make a Big Promise

Capture your audience's attention by making a big, bold promise. Make it a promise they can turn into an actionable item. Some examples:

> *"By the end of this speech you will know the 4 F's for creating fabulous stories your audiences will love to hear time and time again."*
>
> *"Pick up your pencil and get ready! You'll increase your sales by 200% if you follow the 3 C's to Consistent Selling."*
>
> *"By the time we're done today you'll go from being a zero to*

being a hero in all your personal relationships."

It is crucial however, that if you make a big promise you must be able to follow through with it.

Bonus Option

Advanced Option: One that only The Best Speakers even dare to try.

Say Nothing At All

Yes, you are reading it right. Say nothing at all. You have to be really confident to pull this off but it is very powerful. Here's an example:

Opening with Silence

In 2008, while competing in Toastmasters International World Championship of Public Speaking, I decided to open one of my speeches with silence. Every speaker had gone up on stage using a high energy approach during their openings. They wanted to be a little bit like Tony Robbins: high energy, enthusiastic and super confident. I can't really blame them, Tony is one of the greatest speakers on the planet. Their openings sounded something like this:

"Good afternoon everyone. WOW! What a beautiful audience. Isn't this exciting...."

"Hello everyone! Come on I NEED EVERYONE TO SAY HEEEL-LOOOOO...."

Or "HEEEEHAHAAAAA! I SURVIVED CANCER..."

And that's O.K. for Tony Robbins. It's O.K. for thousands of other speakers. It's even O.K. for Toastmasters competing for the world championship. As the Booya Speaker I encourage speakers to be creative with their openings. If everybody is doing the big opening, why not surprise the audience and be silent? Doing the unexpected is a terrific strategy in comedy and in speaking. If you do the expected guess what? You've become a cliché. Ninety percent of the audience will tune you right out.

Do the unexpected. Just stand there for five seconds. Here's the trick, as you stand there, look out into the audience and scan the room. It takes confidence but if you do it you'll have the audience leaning forward in their seats wondering what you'll do next. Having the audience "wondering" is the key to great public speaking.

During the World Championship I shook the chairman's hand after being introduced, walked to the center of the stage, waited for the applause to end and very slowly lifted my right arm and pointed to the ceiling. I held that pose for about five seconds in complete silence, scanned the room and said, "Pretty interesting image isn't it, but this is exactly what Babe Ruth did during the 1932 World Series of Baseball in Chicago. I also believe this image became the symbol of commitment for thousands of Americans. If Babe Ruth could commit to his swing and call his shot, what can you commit to?"

There are two reasons why that opening worked so well. First, it was unexpected. The audience fully expected me to get up there and wow them with my energy, my enthusiasm and my passion. All of which are absolutely necessary in any speech. My approach, however, was just unique enough to make them think, "Hey, this is different. What's he going to do next?" That question is what I keep asking myself when writing and practicing a speech, "What can I do that will surprise or keep the audience interested? How can I deliver this line or that story in a unique way?"

The second reason the silent opening worked so well is because I also ended the speech with it. I wrapped it all up by saying, "The next time you really want to commit to something but feel afraid, I want you to remember Babe Ruth. I want you to remember this…." I then pointed to the sky, holding the pose for about five seconds. From there I looked into their eyes, gave them a little wink and walked off stage. The place erupted with applause. I knew I had connected with my audience. Silent open. Silent close. Silence is big.

BIG OPENING – Things to Remember

As a Booya Speaker your goal is to stand out from the crowd. Booya Speakers aren't afraid to use LOTS of body language. They use every part of the stage, from right to left, back and front. They use their voices. They speak loudly. They speak quietly and they say nothing at all. Booya Speakers think of everyone in the room. Remember, if you are in a big room, people in the back of the room can't see small movement. If you are in a small room your movements don't need to be as big.

During one event I attended, when the speaker was introduced there was silence for a short while. When the speaker started talking there was no one on the stage. Everyone started looking around to see where in the world he was speaking from. He was tossing a ball and talking from the back of the room. His speech was about how opportunities come from unexpected places. The fact that he spoke from an unexpected location really drove the point home. The ball represented opportunity. If you aren't looking, opportunity may come your way and you'll miss it. It was a big opening. Find your big opening.

Here are four more examples you can use to open your speech. They make great openings because they get right to the point, start a great story, or ask the audience to do an activity.

"You may know that I am the top salesmen (insert whatever is right for you), but what you may not know about me is that I suffered from very low esteem for 20 years." (Insert whatever is right for you here.)
"I'd like everyone to stand up and cheer the following cheer

with me..." (Invent a cheer.)

"*I have achieved every goal I set for myself, but I have never...*" (Fill in the blank.)

"*My goal was to become the greatest ball player of all time... instead I become the greatest_______.*" (Fill in the blank.)

With each of these examples you'll take the audience in one direction and then turn on a dime. It's a great way to keep audiences on their toes and listening to every word you say. You can use this technique in your opening and throughout your entire speech.

Body of the Speech

The body of the speech is the meat of your speech. It's where you are going to give all of your information.

In the body of the speech I have found that a personal story is the best way to connect with my audience. I connect by using one or more of the 4 A's. These are:

1. Anecdote
2. Analogy
3. Activity
4. Acronym

Let's look at each of those a little more closely

Anecdote

An anecdote is a lesson being told by using a personal story. To find your best stories I would suggest you use the 4F method. Share you Firsts, Fears, Failures and Frustrations. We'll go over the 4Fs in more detail in a later chapter.

Analogy

You can use an analogy to tell a story. Probably one of the best analogies about drug abuse came from a commercial using eggs. Can you recall seeing the fried eggs as the narrator said the line, "This is your brain. This is your brain on drugs. Any questions? "

Speakers and writers often use one story, event, or sentence (the analogy) to bring home the point they are trying to make within their own personal story. Noah's Ark, for example, is a great analogy about the value of starting over. It may not be easy, there may be a lot of hard work involved but in the end the value of fresh beginnings is immeasurable.

Activity

Doing an activity is another great way to breathe life into your speech. It gets the audience actively engaged in what you are saying. I do a lot of speeches on change management. The following is an example of an activity I use:

I ask audience members to find a partner and stand back to back. I ask them to change **twelve** things about themselves, making sure their partner can't see what they are changing. Of course everyone looks at me and starts to complain. So I quickly say, "O.K., change only two things about yourself," which they always do. I then ask them to face their partner and identify what they changed. I ask them to go back to back again and change two more things, face each other and identify those two things. I ask them to repeat the process one more time. The purpose of the exercise is to show them they could have initially changed twelve items but it was easier to change a little and change often rather than changing twelve items all at once.

Acronym

Using an acronym is a wonderful way of giving a speech. Everybody remembers acronyms. Not only do they remember the acronym but they'll also remember the story you used for each letter of the acronym.

One of my speeches uses the acronym IMPACT. The message of the speech is that it's no longer acceptable to just be an employee anymore. We all have to be leaders in whatever we do.

IMPACT stands for:

Important
Moments
Purpose
Action
Commitment
Teach

With each of those letters I tell a story. At the end of the speech I bring it all together with one sentence, "Now that you understand how the IMPACT acronym works I want you to go home and use this formula to lead a life of maximum IMPACT." They leave with a feeling of hope and a plan of action.

Conclusion

It's amazing how many speakers are afraid to LET their audience know they are finishing. Here's a situation you may find yourself in as a speaker. Let's say you've been talking for about half and hour.

Realistically some people may have lost their train of thought. Some people might be thinking about their grocery list, messages to return or even what Facebook update they'd like to put up. People are likely to remember the first few minutes of your speech and the last couple of minutes of your speech. That's why it's important to let them know you've come to the end of your speech. It helps to bring people back into focus and pay attention to your concluding remarks.

Before you finish your speech here are a few sentences you can use to let your audience know you are about to conclude your speech and bring them back into focus:

"Before I leave here today, I want you to know this……"

"I have 3 minutes left so I'd like you to remember these three points..."

"I've come to the end of my speech. Of all the things I've said here today, I'd like you to remember just this one thing more than anything else…."

What About the Question and Answer Period

You might be asking yourself, "Martin, what if the audience has questions? When do I have a question and answer period?" Great question. You never end with Q & A. The reason you shouldn't is because what if nobody has any questions? Imagine you've just delivered the best speech in human history. Everybody is feeling hopeful about their future. They can't wait to get up and give you a standing ovation and you say, "Are there any questions?" And that's when it happens. Silence. All the wonderful energy has been sucked right out of the room and everybody feels uncomfortable. This is the reason so many people are afraid to make speeches. We all desperately want to avoid the "dead zone."

The opposite might happen. You've just delivered a great

speech and there are twenty questions. You answer the last question and now what? Again, another awkward moment. How do you know it's the last question? Are you finished answering the question? How does the chairperson know you are finished?

I believe the best thing to do is tell the audience what you plan on doing. Here is how I handle it:

"I've come to the end of my speech. How about I take about five questions because I'd like to keep the program on schedule. After the five questions I'll wrap up with one final example about what we've been talking about here today so that we can bring it all together." If there are no questions I'll ask the first one. "I bet you're wondering how I came up with the IMPACT acronym."

This will usually start the questions coming. I've even planted questions in the audience before I even speak. I'll approach a couple of people prior to the speech and ask them to ask one or two questions when the time is right.

Once the Q & A is done I transition to my concluding story. I usually keep it very short, no more than three minutes. The final story is meant to wrap up everything they have learned throughout the presentation. I make sure the energy is really high, everybody feels positive and have a plan of action. Once I say my last sentence I pause and say, "Thank you." For example, I end one speech with, "and that Ladies and Gentlemen is how you too can live a life of tremendous IMPACT. Let me hear you say it one more time ...BOOYA" pause, they do the cheer and I say, "Thank you." That leaves no doubt in anyone's mind that I am done. The emcee or chairperson then comes to greet me onstage. I can already hear some speakers saying, "I never end with a thank you. I just finish my last sentence and take a bow." If it works for them, that's great. The reason I end with a "thank you" is because I didn't say my thank you's at the start. I think it's just common courtesy to thank the audience for coming out as well as whoever else you feel like thanking.

The key to your conclusion is to leave your audience tremendously hopeful, energized and with a clear sense of direction. Too many times I see speakers exit the stage and the audience is left wondering, "O.K., what do I do now?" They feel good, they feel energized but they have no idea what their next step should be.

During one my speeches I say the following:

"I now want you to go home and write down on a piece of paper what is Important to you, what Action you will take each day to reach your goal and how you can Give back."

You can ask them to read three books, apply for another job by next week, or write just 500 words a day to complete their book. Just make sure to give them a clear and definable action item. Did you notice I used three items? I'm a big believer in using the rule of 3's in almost every situation that I want to make a point or teach something important. One is not enough, two is good and four is overkill. Three is just right.

How to Handle a Standing Ovation

Stand there. That's right, just stand there, mouth the words "Thank You" and walk off just as the clapping starts to wind down. I've seen speakers walk off just when the standing ovation is starting up or right in the middle. The audience needs to show their appreciation. Let them show it.

What If You Don't Get a Standing Ovation

If you don't get a Standing O clearly the audience wasn't listening and should be ashamed of themselves. Kidding aside, generally you won't get a standing ovation. There are several reasons: it's not appropriate for the situation, not the goal of the speech, the room might have been hot, or they might have been a low key group. I've yet to see accountants or engineers stand up for anybody. They will, however, be the first ones to approach you at the back of the room and tell you how much they enjoyed your presentation.

The goal of speaking is not to get standing ovations. The goal is to reach your audience, make them think and perhaps even change. I've also heard a number of speakers say they don't speak for standing ovations but rather for standing invitations. This means they speak so they will be invited back time and time again. Now that is power. It also happens to be the best way to make a living as a speaker.

Chapter 2

Turning a Good Speech into an OUTSTANDING Speech

Now that you know how to create the essential parts to your speech you'll now learn how to make it truly outstanding. While audiences may vaguely remember a good speech, they may not remember the most significant points three days after the speech. I call this the water cooler test. People often talk around the water cooler at work and chat about the weekend, upcoming vacations, or their kids. I try to picture them talking about my presentation. What can I do and say so they'll remember my speech and talk about it around the water cooler? If my audience can remember my main points three days after I give a speech, I know I have given an outstanding speech. I try to go one step further. I often ask audience members that I see much later on if they remember the stories I told, the names of the characters I used and why the story was relevant. If I gave an outstanding speech they will remember all of these things. I'm hoping they will even remember my energy as a speaker. I want the audience to remember my movements on stage. They will also hopefully vividly remember the parts of the speech that touched them and the parts that made them laugh.

As a speaker, what do you want to be remembered as? Will it be as someone who had a good speech or someone who gave an outstanding speech? In this chapter I'm going to give you some top tips on how to turn a good speech into a truly OUTSTANDING speech.

Always Use Characters

The first step is to think about the use of characters. Characters are vital to any good story. It's all in the details. It can't be, "There was a girl with blond hair." It has to be, "There was a cute freckle-faced girl with blond braids down to her waist. Her name was Lucy, but her name sounded way too nice for the mischievous twinkle in her gray-green eyes." You must bring your characters to life. Include things like:

- A name
- What they look like—in detail
- What they smell like

Not surprisingly characters are usually people. They can, however, also be the soul, spirit, or some other inanimate object. I've used my guitar as a character. I'm the worst guitar player in the world but my guitar speaks to me and tells me not to give up.

Here is an example from one of my speeches describing a character:

I can clearly remember the first day JT walked into my office. I figured he was about my age, 23. He was about 6'2", weighed no more than 180 pounds, very slight for someone that tall. His clothes were tattered and he didn't smell all that good either. I could tell JT was a broken man. He stretched out his long arm, his rough hand grabbed a hold of mine and he said in a deep voice,
"Are you Martin Presse?"
I said, "Yes I am."
He quickly said, "Good, I hear you teach people how to read. Is that true?"
"As a matter of fact I do."
He smiled and said, "Good, I want you to teach me how to read."
His voice was clear and powerful. This was a man on a mission.

You immediately get a sense of who JT is. He's probably had a rough life, he doesn't look or smell very good, but I also think you get a sense that he wants to make a change and is quite determined to do so.

To take it one step further, this would be an ideal time to invite the audience into your story. This is an opportune time to make it relevant to them and do a check in. I'm willing to bet many speakers would just keep going with this story. One of the most important things to remember when telling a story/speech is to always make it relevant to the audience. I'll repeat this sentence several times throughout the book. What does it mean to make a speech relevant to the audience? It means doing what I just did. I asked you a question. I made you think. I focused on you. The worst thing you can do is tell your story and repeat, Me, Myself and I throughout your presentation. The audience can only hear you talk about yourself for so long. The audience may not consciously be thinking "Man, this guy sure is talking about himself a lot. I wonder when he'll start to focus on me?" but they are thinking about it on a subconscious level. Every few minutes you have to do what I call a "check in" by asking a "you" focused question.

As a Booya Speaker you'll take this opportunity to ask the audience a question or two.

"Have you ever met someone like JT?" Long pause. "How do you think you would have responded to someone like him? I'll be honest with you, he made me nervous. He was tough and mean looking. Would you have been able to look past the exterior? I had a really hard time doing that. Within two weeks, however, he had won me over completely."

Use the power of "You" in your speeches. It will change the way audiences connect with you dramatically. You'll also get rebooked time and time again.

Dialogue

Once you have your characters, you have to give them dialogue. Dialogue is FAR more compelling than the alternative, which is narrative. It has much more impact. It can be between two characters, yourself or even with inanimate objects. Which one do you think sounds better?

Alex sat down next to me after a particularly rough hockey game. He knew I was upset about the game being so hard on him. He told me he really loved hockey and that he enjoyed the roughness of the game. He felt it was exciting. He wasn't afraid to get hurt. He said he felt really involved in the action whenever the game became very physical and that I shouldn't be afraid that he would get injured. He made it very clear that he could take care of himself even against the bigger kids.

Or

Alex sat down next to me after a particularly rough hockey game. He knew I was upset about the game being so hard on him. After a few moments he spoke up, "Dad, you know I love hockey more than anything. I want you to know I can take care of myself out there. The rougher it gets, the more I like it. I might fall down, take a hard hit, but I'll get back up, laugh it off and get right back in the game. You have to let me enjoy this. I love it. I absolutely love it."

What could I say? I turned to him, smiled and said, "It's my job to worry. I'm your dad now go get me a hot chocolate. I'm freezing."

I'm willing to bet you think the example with the dialogue is better. Audiences also tend to remember how something was said much more than what was said. It's for this reason that your voice should reflect your emotions. In the example I used above, when I speak as Alex, I speak slowly and softly, I don't smile. My voice and body language match the mood of the moment. The value of good dialogue explains why people remember how they felt the first time someone said, "I love you" or "We're through." They'll talk in detail about what happened afterwards because of the feelings that are attached to those moments. People generally connect with and remember emotions first and facts second. Booya Speakers use the power of emotion to get their point across. Once your emotion, passion and purpose are conveyed using dialogue, audiences will follow you anywhere.

Some of the most compelling dialogue you will ever have is the dialogue you have with yourself. Let the audience hear your inner dialogue. Here's an example:

Right before I walked out of my hotel room to speak in front of 2500 people I looked in the mirror. I said out loud, "boy...you are in trouble." Oddly enough it was as if the image spoke back, "Listen, you've dreamed of this moment your whole life. Do you want to be "that guy", the guy who quit, the guy who people will say, "oh Martin, he's the guy who made it to the finals and quit." Martin this is your chance to show your kids how important it it to push through despite being afraid...forget about yourself and be "that guy", the guy who does the thing that needs to get done.

Create a Scene and Appeal To Their Senses

Now that you have characters and have given them a powerful voice with great dialogue you must now place your characters in a scene to have the dialogue in. Describe the scene exactly as it would be. Describe what you heard, smelled, touched, saw and tasted. Be as specific as you can to appeal to your audiences senses.

People are deeply connected with their senses. For example, I dated a beautiful young woman named Christine when I was seventeen years old, over twenty years ago, and every time I hear George

Michaels' song "One More Try" I am instantly back on the dance floor where we first kissed. I can still smell her perfume and the feel of my hand on the small of her back.

The most frequent question I get is, "How and when do I move on stage?" Great question. You move among the different scenes you create on stage. Doing so will give you a reason to move, to use your hands and to use the entire stage area. For example when I talk about my father's last days I describe the hospital room, the position of the bed within the room, the monitors and where my brothers and sister stayed for hours during the week he passed away. On the other side of the stage is the cafeteria where we sat and discussed what my father would want us to do in this situation. The middle of the stage is reserved for moments when I speak directly to the audience, when I step outside my scenes and ask the "you" focused questions.

The stage is also a great timeline. The area going to the audience's right is the future and the area to their left is the past. When I talk about being a child I also stand on the audience's left hand side of the stage. As I talk about becoming a man I move towards their right. When I move across the stage the audience sees me moving towards the future.

Humor

While it can be tempting to just "add a joke", it's not a good idea. Instead, uncover the humor. There is humor in just about everything. I've heard many comedians say "Humor is just tragedy plus time." This means almost any situation given enough time can potentially be humorous. People may not think their lost luggage, divorce, or bankruptcy is funny, but given enough time any of those scenarios can be uproariously funny. My personal preference is to find humor in the dialogue I have with myself or with my characters. If you add humor like you add sprinkles to the top of cookie, audiences will see right through it. Generally, it won't work because they'll see you are trying to get a laugh. If you let the humor come out naturally, like sugar is an ingredient in the cookie, audiences will just follow along with you, enjoying the moment as it happens. Humor can be tough and very subjective. You will get better at finding humor the more you speak and the more confident you become. Over time you'll find what works for you. It's definitely a confidence thing. Here are six tips to help you uncover humor.

1) **Be willing to laugh at your own laugh lines, even if you have delivered the same line 500 times.** If you know a line has worked with friends, on the phone, or at work, definitely bring it into your speech.

2) **Be willing to test your material without telling your friends you are testing it on them.** For example, I started singing like Elvis at the office one day. Both people in my area started laughing. Guess what? I now sing like Elvis in my speeches when I tell a story about putting my daughter to sleep at night. It gets a laugh because it's such a poor imitation.

3) **What you think is sad will often be funny to others.** I have a friend who was once arrested for check fraud. The sheriff showed up at her door, she had to call a friend to come watch her daughter, she was trucked off to jail, spent time in a cellblock with sixty hardened criminals and served about five days of jail time before the judge realized it was all a horrible mistake. As she told me the story she used a sad voice. I couldn't help but laugh. She said, "What's so funny?" She was really upset. I told her to look at herself in the mirror and see if she matched the look of a hardened criminal. She's a beautiful blond, athletic woman with an MBA. She owned a business and it was sheer bad luck and a series of unfortunate events that led her to jail. I begged her to tell the story to some friends and watch their reaction. She got laughs. When she told the same story to a large audience, she got huge laughs.

4) **Go in the opposite direction the audience thinks you will go.**

For example, I tell a story about how I wanted to show off a little bit in front of friends while sitting in a restaurant that happened to have a poster of me. It was a poster promoting an up coming show I was in. I sat down next to a woman in her late 70's and said, "What do you think of that young fellow in the poster?"
She responded, "Oh he's quite handsome."
I said, "Do you think he looks like me at all."
She replied, "Oh, no! Not at all. He's much younger and better looking." Booya! She got me. Huge laughs from the audience.

5)   **Take yourself off the pedestal. The late Johnny Carson was the greatest.** Nobody can touch Johnny. One of the reasons he remains a legend is because he took himself off the pedestal. If ever he made a mistake or delivered a line that no body got, he was the first to laugh at himself. He was simply the best at being self-effacing.

6)   Don't tell jokes. Enough said.

The Conflict

The hook to any speech is the story, but the hook to any story is the conflict. The movie "Titanic" is a great example. It's a great story with a great message—never quit. Against all odds you never quit. During the movie the conflict just kept escalating. The water kept rising. There weren't enough lifeboats. It was dark. The water was freezing. The tension just kept rising to unbearable levels.

As a speaker one of your jobs is to keep the tension rising, just like in the movie Titanic, Independence Day or even Ground Hog Day.... As the tension rises the audience will slowly lean in wondering what will happen next and who will say what. Your role is to keep them guessing, thinking, and questioning the entire time you speak. If you speak about sales, tell them stories about a tough sell (conflict) and how you overcame all the obstacles. If you speak on leadership, share stories about those who refused to follow or the leaders who refused to lead. As a speaking coach I talk about clients who started out not being very good but who grew into magnificent story tellers, making powerful points and changing the lives of thousands. Some clients were much tougher to work with than others. As a speaker I often tell audiences about my early years. There were a lot of missteps and do-over's. The conflict in those early days was mostly with myself, my energy wasn't always very positive.

Conflict can happen in three different ways:

- Man vs. man
- Man vs. self
- Man vs. nature

You can use any of these. You just need to get to the conflict quickly. In the first ninety seconds if possible. It gives the audience a reason to pay attention.

Foundational Phrases

Foundational phrases are probably the most powerful tool you have at your disposal to make an impact during your speeches. They are the sentences audiences will remember weeks, months and even years after your presentation. Essentially, they are the message of the speech said in ten words or less. Here are some famous examples:

- Ask not what your country can do for you, but what you can do for your country.
- When you know better, you'll do better.
- We are the change that we seek.

Typically, foundational phrases must follow these three simple rules:

- Fewer than ten words
- Should have rhyme and rhythm
- Must be easily remembered.

There are always exceptions to those rules. Early on I used phrases that didn't always have rhyme and rhythm. I used to say, "Commit to your swing." Now I say, "You have got to commit to you swing. When you commit, you won't quit." Instead of saying "I believe in you," I now say, "I believe in you. Do you believe in you?" My initial foundational phrases worked well, but I've noticed an even better reaction to the new phrases.

Chapter 3

4 F's to Finding Great Stories

Where do speech ideas come from?

I used to sit at my kitchen table, go for long walks, or even drive for hours hoping to find inspiration. While working with my speaking coach, Craig Valentine, I asked him that very same question, "Craig, where do you get your ideas from? You seem to have countless great stories! How do you do it?"

The answer was remarkably simple — but then again, Craig has a way of making speaking look so easy. He said, "Martin, if you look for your <u>firsts</u>, your <u>fears</u>, your <u>frustrations</u>, and your <u>failures</u>, you'll come up with incredible stories audiences will connect with time and time again." After thinking about it for a bit, I realized that Craig was, once again, correct.

In mid-March 2008, two weeks before a very important speech, I sat down at my kitchen table and realized I didn't have a good speech. The audience was expecting something great. All I had was something mediocre. For some reason I do my best thinking while driving. So, I got in my car and drove six hours East—no radio, just my thoughts and a full tank of gasoline. Suddenly it hit me! *Firsts, Fears, Frustrations, and Failures.*" Within ten minutes I had the speech I was looking for.

Throughout this chapter you'll see the word "connect" numerous times. As speakers we typically want to connect with our audience quickly. To "connect" means to have audience members lean forward in their seats, nod their heads approvingly, or give some other indication that shows they're emotionally connected to what you have to say. You'll connect quickly by using the 4F's. Here they are in more detail.

Firsts

Everybody experiences "Firsts." Share a number of your firsts with audiences and watch the connection build. Here's an example:

"I can clearly remember the first time I teed off during a golf tournament. I was nine years old. More than 200 people surrounded the tee off box and my coach, eighty-year-old Mrs. Carpenter, stood just a few feet away. I was so nervous! My hands shook, I could barely breathe and the ball seemed like a tiny white speck of dust. Have you ever been that nervous? Maybe it was on graduation day and you were the class valedictorian. Or, how about on your wedding day? Maybe it was your first job interview? We've all experienced many firsts."

With this example, I established a connection with the audience by sharing a "First." They know I've been there, nervous just like them. In this particular speech I go on and relate how I failed miserably to hit the ball when teeing off. Not only did I miss it once, but twice! It went no more than 12 feet both times. I was nervous and it showed. Generally, I get a lot of laughs when telling this story. For some time I couldn't understand why I got the laughs and then it hit me, they were laughing at their own first! They were reliving their own failure and now that they had put some time between them and the experience, they could see the humor in it.

Fear

If you plan to share some of your "Firsts" you will inevitably talk about the second F: "Fear." Everybody understands fear. We've all had to face "the fear," as my son likes to call it. Quite often, the lesson comes from how we handled our fear. I'm sure you can come up with three stories that involve fear. How about facing a bully, a car accident, or fear of losing a job? The trick is to identify the right kind of fear. Telling an audience you're afraid of spiders might not make the same deep emotional impact as telling them you're afraid to fail, to experience new things, or to lose at love.

I often tell a story about spending the first nineteen years of my life running from bullies, but there was one person who really had my number. The mere mention of his name gave me the chills. I would have trouble breathing and basically became paralyzed. Eventually the day came when he cornered my friends and me at the end of a long hallway at the local hockey rink. There was nowhere to run except through him and twelve of his friends. For a moment I thought I was lucky because he walked up to my close friend, Harold, and they started talking back and forth. Within seconds, I realized it wasn't friendly talk and they were about to come to blows.

Suddenly, I became enraged. Something deep within me cried out, "If you don't step in now, you'll never step in. If ever there was a moment to be great this is it. Step in!!!" And I did, right in between the two of them. I stood nose-to-chest with the guy who had me running for more than a year. The words just flowed out from me as if it were somebody else talking.

"I am sick and tired of running. I am sick and tired of you and your friends coming after me just because I speak a different language. (They spoke French and I spoke English.) If you want to fight, we'll have a fight right here, just you and me. When you're done beating me up, then it'll be all over. I am done running. Do you want all your friends to watch you beating on someone half your size, or do you want to shake my hand and be the bigger man?"

I was sure he was about to slug me right then and there, but he didn't. I was stunned! He stepped back and laughed. We all started laughing. He never did shake my hand, but he did walk away shaking his head. That was good enough for me. I have rarely been afraid since that day. That was my dragon. What's your dragon? Is it time for you to step in?

I use that particular story a great deal. And every time I use it, I hear the comment, "WOW! It was like I was right there with you at the rink. I got bullied too, Martin!" They go on and tell me their own story. Fear is a powerful motivator for change. I suggest you use it a great deal to help your audience change their present circumstance.

Failure

Fear and the third F, "Failure", are close cousins. They are often used in the same sentence and certainly in the same story. I separate the two because I truly believe that if you have lived, you have failed at least once. If you have failed, you have a story to tell. People tend to remember their failures in intricate detail. I remember being inches away from bankruptcy in 1998. I had $100 left to my name, owed $15,000 in credit card bills and couldn't pay the rent. To lower my living expenses I ate massive quantities of rice and stole toilet paper out of office buildings. Is that too much information? It might be, but I'm doing it to make a point: people remember their failures.

Sharing your failures, however, is just the beginning. I've noticed over time that speakers who laugh at their failures make a tremendous impact on the audiences. Once I started using this method I noticed that I got a lot more laughs and created a much deeper connection with my audience. When you speak, go ahead and laugh at your failures. It shows the audience two things. First it shows that you were able to overcome adversity and second, it takes you off the pedestal. I've mentioned already the importance of showing how comparable you are with your audience. They have to know you aren't perfect.

When I talk about my bankruptcy I get huge laughs because I also tell the audience I wore a very expensive three-piece suit, drove a very nice car and stole only the very best toilet paper: three-ply. I focus on the humorous life lessons I learned during that time. For example, buying a business when you don't know the difference between profit and income probably means you shouldn't be in business. If your business partner says, "Selling is overrated," you probably shouldn't go into business with that person. And, if your accountant says, "Your business partner is paying himself $12,500/month while you're borrowing on your credit cards to pay the rent," you might want to re-evaluate your position.

Frustration

"Frustration" is the final F. It's an emotion we all feel. The same method applies here. I suggest you go back in time and share a story that illustrates why you felt frustrated and what you learned from that experience. Here's an example:

I grew up playing tennis. I cannot remember a day when I wasn't holding a tennis racket. My heroes were Bjorn Borg, John McEnroe and Jimmy Connors. My best friend Paul and I loved tennis so much we pretended to attend Wimbledon when the tournament was on TV. My mom was so incredible. She would even serve us Breakfast at Wimbledon, strawberries and ice cream. For years, Paul and I would practice together and compete against one another—and for years, I was the victor.

Suddenly it happened. Paul beat me. It probably happened on a sunny Sunday afternoon, the temperature hovering around 33 degrees Celsius, both of us aged sixteen. Game, Set and Match to Paul. What happened? Just a bad day I suppose. Those bad days started happening more and more often. You might be thinking, "What's the big deal? It's just tennis!" At the time, however, tennis was my life and nothing was more frustrating than losing at tennis. I was beating the more seasoned players in my small home town. Tennis made me a somebody. Losing to Paul made me an anybody. Over the next two years, Paul began to beat me on a regular basis, then on a daily basis, and eventually it was hopeless to even try. As frustrating as that was I learned one of the most valuable lessons of my life during those final two years of tennis. In life, there will always be somebody who will get the better of you. It's not personal, it's not for lack of trying, it just is. That lesson served me well as I became a university student. If I saw someone who was better than me in a particular subject, I sought out his help. As a professional speaker, if I see someone who connects better than I do, rather than let myself become frustrated by my situation, I quickly seek the speaker out and figure how she does it.

As you can see the 4F's are a wonderful way to find all those great stories that lie within you, just waiting to be given new life. When people ask why I share such personal stories, I think they're actually saying, "Why do you use the 4F method?" The answer is simple. Audiences want to know that you're like them. If you're special they won't relate to you. You don't want audiences to place you on a pedestal, if they do you'll have lost your ability to connect. By sharing your firsts, fears, frustrations, and failures, you'll be reachable, touchable and you'll have placed yourself on a level that the audience can truly connect with!

Chapter 4

Dealing with The Dreaded Jitters

Everyone and I mean EVERYONE gets the jitters. Whether it's your first speech or your ten thousandth speech. It's not a bad thing. It means you're alive and that sure beats the alternative. If you aren't nervous it means you don't care. If you don't care, I guarantee you, you'll be less than your very best.

Now, there is a difference between being nervous and having the jitters so badly that you stutter or pass out. Here are a few tried and true ways to get your nerves under a modicum of control.

Stretch

Stretching is a wonderful thing. It relaxes the muscles and the mind at the same time. I strongly suggest looking online at some basic yoga moves or picking up a book on yoga. If you have the time, try taking a couple of classes. You'll learn to stretch and relax those tense muscles.

If it's not yoga at least do some basic stretching. Especially your neck and shoulders which tend to tense up when you are under stress. Then move all the way down the body. Also, sit on the floor and touch your fingers to your toes to stretch your back out. You'll be glad you did after your speech.

Incantations and Visualization

Here comes the Tony Robins in me. I'm not going to shy away from this section because incantations and visualization techniques work. I firmly believe one of thc biggest reasons I was able to get up in front of large audiences long before I had the necessary experience is because I've been visualizing myself in front of thousands since I was nine. I started doing "power talks" or incantations in my mid-twenties when I realized I had horrible self-talk. Hundreds of times a day I would give myself terrible messages like, "Martin, you're so stupid. You're so slow, nobody will ever love you. What an idiot." Day in and day out my mind would process these messages. No wonder I was miserable for most of my life.

Fortunately, I was able to hide my misery from most people. Somebody, however, caught on and recommended I read a book by Tony Robbins. I can't remember exactly which book it was but I remember reading a section on "self talk" and that with some effort I could change the way I spoke to myself. Each time I caught myself saying something negative about myself I had to say something positive one hundred times over. Initially I thought this was ridiculous but I gave it a shot. One of the things I noticed right away was that I had the absolute worst internal dialogue. I never gave myself a pat on the back for anything. Once I dedicated myself to changing my self talk I became fanatical about it. All I would do whenever I wasn't involved in a conversation with someone was repeat this little phrase, "I'm smart, popular and people like me. I'm smart, popular, and people like me. I'm smart, popular and people like me." I chose this sentence because it was easy to remember and rolled off the tongue quickly. I said it thousands of times a day. It soon changed to, "I'm smart, fun, focused and full of energy."

Combine positive self-talk with powerful visual imagery and you will find yourself with more self-esteem and creative energy than you ever thought possible. The biggest audience I ever faced was 2,500.

When I looked up and saw the sea of faces I felt right at home, nervous, but right at home. I had seen these faces thousands of times before. I sincerely hope you practice incantations and visualization techniques. It has changed mine and will change your life immeasurably.

Breathing Exercises

It sounds crazy but you'd be amazed how many people forget to breathe when they are nervous. The exercise is simple: breath in, hold it for 5 seconds and breath out slowly. Focus solely on breathing. Initially, you might feel like you'll pass out. If you do feel light-headed then try holding your breath for shorter periods of time. The trick is to breath. It sounds so simple and ridiculous but it works. If you get nervous focusing on your breathing will help bring your wits about you very quickly.

Vocal Exercises

Even the pros still do their vocal exercises. If you've never done any vocal exercises, you can look up vocal exercises on YouTube and find a variety to choose from. It's a little difficult to describe vocal exercises in written form so I recommend you look up drills on You-Tube.

Focus on the Speech Itself

Even if you have a teleprompter available, and most of the time you won't, it is vital that you KNOW your speech. This doesn't mean you have to memorize your speech word for word. Have you ever seen a speaker get stuck on a word or a line and they just can't seem to get it out? It's probably because they've tried really hard to memorize it. View the speech as being several small parts. It will have a beginning, middle and an end. Each section will have a story or perhaps an activity. Your job is to remember what story you've attached to each section. The majority of your focus should be on your stories and how they enhance the point you are trying to make.

I'm not saying you shouldn't spend hours practicing. You absolutely need to spend time rehearsing your speech, whether it's a ten minute presentation or a ninety minute keynote.

I recall a speaker telling me he had decided not to rehearse his speech too much because he wanted it to sound natural. What happened was tragic. He sounded completely unnatural because he wasn't sure what he wanted to say next. He hadn't gone through his stories enough to know exactly what his message was. He wasn't sure where to stand, where to really punch a word or line. He didn't pause because of his nerves. He ran through his ten minute speech in under eight minutes and left the audience wondering what his message really was.

Everybody practices at different time intervals. I rarely practice more than one hour a day. I take small chunks and rehearse them for sixty minutes. If I do that for seven days I know I can speak for ninety minutes without notes. I know some speakers who practice for ten minutes four or five times a day. Try different methods and see what works for you.

The Opening and the Close

These are truly the most vital parts. Make sure you know them without fault. Even if you mess up in between, if your audience remembers the opening and the close, they'll still remember you as a strong outstanding speaker.

The General Direction

As I've said before, you don't necessarily have to know the whole speech by heart, but you do need to know the general direction.

Once you get into the speech, little parts may change and extra parts may come to you. That's O.K., as long as you stay with the general direction.

Make sure you know your main points and the stories which are associated with each point. The stories may grow and change slightly each time you tell them. Again, no big deal. As long as they sound real and authentic, you'll be fine.

Video or Audio Tape your Speech

It's amazing what annoying habits you find out you have when you watch or hear yourself. It's a hard thing to sit through, but I highly encourage you to do it from time to time. It will definitely make you cognizant of all the little annoying things you do and will keep you from doing them in the future. One of the things I learned about myself is that I often speak too quickly, especially when I am jazzed up about my topic. I need to contain my enthusiasm. I would never have noticed had I not taped my live speeches.

Chapter 5

What is The Audience Thinking?

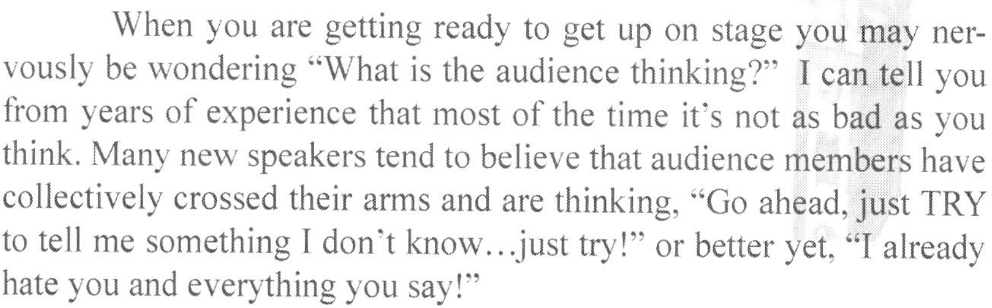

When you are getting ready to get up on stage you may nervously be wondering "What is the audience thinking?" I can tell you from years of experience that most of the time it's not as bad as you think. Many new speakers tend to believe that audience members have collectively crossed their arms and are thinking, "Go ahead, just TRY to tell me something I don't know…just try!" or better yet, "I already hate you and everything you say!"

Here's the truth:

1.)   The audience wants you to be successful.

2.)   They want you to teach them something.

3.)   They want to have a wonderful experience.

Use that positive energy to your advantage. If someone has "that smirk" don't look at him again. Simply focus on the enthusiastic people that are the 99.9% of your audience.

What About Tough Audiences?

Let's face it, there will be times when you have a tough audience. A tough audience doesn't necessarily mean you have a room full of hecklers. Generally the only time you'll face hecklers is in a bar. I have never had someone try to interrupt or distract me while speaking at a conference, a business meeting or even a wedding. I once saw another speaker deal with someone who tried to debate every point the speaker made. It was clear to the speaker that everyone in the room was annoyed with this person. Eventually the speaker said it was time for a short five minute break, she pulled the person aside and said she would meet with him personally after the meeting if he promised to stop interrupting the session. The stranger got the hint and the little bit of attention he wanted. The speaker went back on stage and performed wonderfully.

What If Nobody In The Room Has Any Energy...Now What?

The BOOYA Technique

The tough audiences I'm referring to are the ones with no energy. Typically they've just eaten, haven't eaten, or it's late in the day. You can take charge of the situation with the right attitude. For years I would leave after a bad presentation saying to myself or the event organizer, "Too bad they had such low energy. Not my fault I couldn't get them excited about the material. Oh well, maybe next year." Most of the time there was no next year for me. That client went out and found another speaker. Eventually I learned to have a different mindset: If the audience seems disengaged, unresponsive and tired, I make a conscious decision to do whatever it takes to change their unresponsive nature and make them pay attention, to really listen and learn something of value. Here is one way I handle the situation when my audience lacks energy. I make them all stand up. I tell them (in my most excited voice), "Okay, we need a little more energy in this room. Now, I want everyone to give me a BOOYA." Inevitably, the first BOOYA is a little weak. It's to be expected. So I tell them. "Okay, that was...mildly... okay (laughter)... I know you can do a little better. Give me another... BOOYA." And they usually come back with a stronger BOOYA. It's just a fun word to say and you can feel the energy increase. So I have them do it ONE MORE time and BOY does that final BOOYA increase the energy in the room. I firmly believe that action affects emotion. If you get your audience moving, their emotions will follow right along. Maybe BOOYA works for you or maybe you'll find your own word that fits YOUR personality and brings the energy into your room. Find what works for you.

If you ever see Tony Robbins speaking you'll notice he has people clapping and dancing every half hour and Tony can speak five hours straight because of that technique. He gets people physically involved in his programs to keep them emotionally and mentally tuned in.

If the audience is tough because you've said something inappropriate I would suggest apologizing. Do not act like you haven't said or done anything wrong. In all likelihood you know you said something inappropriate and they know you said something inappropriate. There is no point ignoring the pink elephant in the room. If you are toasting the bride and groom and have crossed the line you will in all likelihood not be able to get them back on your side so you may as well apologize, finish what you were talking about and leave the stage.

There are a number of speakers who will tell you never to apologize to an audience. I agree, never apologize for taking a stand or having an opinion. Do apologize if you've insulted somebody, end your speech and exit the stage.

Make Your Audience Feel TALL

Earlier we talked about using acronyms as a tool to create an outstanding speech. If you think you're going to have a tough audience or if you are really nervous I'd like you to remember this acronym: TALL. It stands for Think, Act, Laugh and Learn. I have to credit to Ed Tate, 2000 World Champion of Public Speaking for this acronym. Visit his website and consider getting some coaching from him. He's a tremendously gifted speaker.

Think

Force your audience to evaluate their current belief systems. For instance Rosa Parks is one of my personal heroes. She is a great example of someone who stood by her beliefs, withstood tremendous pressure to conform and taught us all that you don't have to be rich or famous to change the world. I can see it in their eyes as I talk about Rosa Parks. Many in the audience think about what they would have done had they been in her shoes.

Act

Go back to chapter one and review the activity on Change. The activity doesn't have to be big. Getting everyone to cheer Booya is often enough to raise the energy level in the room. Another terrific option is to have mini breakout sessions. You can always ask your audience to break out into groups of two or three and come up with the answer to a question you just asked.

Laugh

You have to make your audience laugh. Yes, this IS a skill that can be worked on. One of the best ways to get your audience to laugh is to do the unexpected. I highly recommend the book "Stand Up Comedy" by Judy Carter. If you aren't naturally funny don't force it. Ask friends and family to help you. You'll be surprised how funny you are by not trying to be funny. If you are telling a story the comedy will come out via the situations you describe and the communication that was had between the characters. Review the six tips on humor I described in chapter two.

Learn

You need to teach your audience something. The caveat is that it has to be REAL content as opposed to what I call "soft content."

There are only half a dozen speakers in the world who can make a living telling their audience that happiness is found in a sunset. Unless you have led a nation through devastation or have led millions in a religious movement you will have to find "concrete content". It has to be real, tangible material such as showing an audience three ways to open a speech, four ways to close a sale, or how to write a book in thirty days.

When teaching or telling a story, if you make your audience Think, Act, Laugh and Learn you'll find that even the toughest audiences will love and appreciate all that you've done. How can they not like you?

Chapter 6

How Do I Practice?

A question I get asked all the time is "Martin…How do I practice?" I have a method that is based on exaggeration. I think many speakers don't have enough vocal variety and body language. It's comes down to not showing enough emotion. If you're going to show emotion, you have to be willing to GO BIG! Going Big is part of the Booya Speaker mentality.

What does "Going Big" mean? When I practice in the living room I practice taking BIG steps, making larger arm motions and exaggerating my facial expressions. I know if I do this during practice, I'll do it live. If I stand still in my living room, I'll stand still on stage. Remember that you have to be bigger on stage, so practice being bigger. It's easier to bring it down a notch when you're live than it is to bring it up a notch so practice being bigger.

If you want to have an interesting learning experience, pay close attention to "non-captivating" speakers. Look very closely at what they do. They tend to be very still, not use their hands at all and their voices have no inflection. They convey very little energy.. That is what you DO NOT want to do. It's a great learning lesson! Remember, Booya Speakers have tremendous energy.

AFTER you watch a non-captivating speaker, watch a really GREAT speaker. My favorites are Craig Valentine, Tony Robins and

Les Brown and Darren LaCroix. Watch what they do. Pay careful attention to their body language, their facial expressions and their energy. Emulate that energy!

Here are some great speakers to watch:

- Craig Valentine
- James Malinchak
- Brendon Burchard
- Les Brown

Albert Mensah
Tony Robins (of course)
Sheryl Roush
Darren LaCroix

Each of them has their own unique style and each is tremendously successful.

Learn to use your eyes to make your points. Look at someone in the audience, hold their gaze when making an important point. Much of your emotion will come via your eyes. They are indeed the windows to the soul. I recall telling an audience about a time when I yelled at my son in front of his friends. Purely by accident I caught a young women's eye as I said, "The little boy I yelled at was my son." The young lady became every person in the audience. They all lived that moment though her. I never forgot that lesson. If you connect with one person you are very likely to connect with most of your audience.

Become comfortable standing still. This may seem a little odd after everything I have just said regarding having energy but there is indeed tremendous power and energy in stillness. You've probably seen war movies where the general stands before his men saying nothing for a few moments, carefully considering his next words. Consider yourself a general before your audience. Stand straight, look them in the eye, let them lean in desperately needing to hear your very first word. Don't move just for movements' sake. You don't want to become a "pacer." Don't be one of those people on stage that looks like a caged animal. They end up making the audience nervous just watching them. Learn to be comfortable standing still. Especially when you are making an important point. I learned this very important lesson while speaking in Billings, Montana in 2010. I gave a speech about how to find fabulous stories using the 4F method. I was telling stories and pacing from the right side of the stage to the left side, back and forth, for forty-five minutes. Lance Miller, 2005 World Champion of Public Speaking, happened to be in the audience that night. After the speech, feeling quite proud of myself, I approached Lance and asked for this feedback. He liked my energy but suggested I slow down on my pacing, not to eliminate it, but to make sure I made a point, stood still for a few seconds, and then moved on physically as well as verbally to my next point. I gave the same speech in Seattle, Washington two months later to tremendous applause. The difference was my controlled pacing. I made sure to pay attention to every part of the room. The audience found the speech far more compelling because I slowed down and looked at them directly when I made an important point.

As much as I preach about being big you must vary your voice and emotions. As a speaker you shouldn't come across as always high energy or always low energy. An always high speaker seems hyperactive or too enthusiastic. An always low speaker comes across as depressed or boring. You have to mix it up for your audience to help them pay attention and understand your message.

Video and audio tape yourself if you really want to see the good, the bad and the ugly. Be prepared!! It won't be fun to watch – in fact it can be downright painful. I recall the first few times I saw myself on camera after doing a speech. I noticed I spoke to quickly and looked at the floor a lot. I still record my live speeches but now I also record my living room rehearsals. By recording yourself you'll quickly pinpoint what changes you can make. It's interesting, what you think is a BIG movement may not look so big on camera or to an audience. You may find you need to exaggerate it even more. You may think you over do emotion, but you need to ramp it up even more. Video and audio will be your best friend...really!

Chapter 7

Data Dumps

What are data dumps? When you hear a speaker talk about very detailed and specific areas of their industry, you're potentially hearing a "data dump." Every type of person and profession can fall into the data dump trap. A finance person would share dozens of detailed graphs on the company's performance. A nurse will discuss every minor detail about patient protocol and a business analyst will analyze every bit of data about profit and loss.

Avoid data dumps as much as you possibly can. There is a small percentage of the population who enjoy speakers that get up and rattle off a bunch of statistics and data. If you're a speaker whose speech contains a large amount of data, facts and figures, such as an accountant, engineer or doctor, there is a way to make your data interesting. Your responsibility as a Booya Speaker is to bring energy to your material, really make it come to life. Booya Speakers appreciate the value of a great story. Using real life examples to highlight your information will be far more memorable. If you rattle off numbers for forty-five minutes…your audience might remember the first thirty seconds, the last thirty seconds…and that's about it.

If you're going to use data to make your points really hit home I suggest wrapping your data around a real life example. I really believe if you use a story you'll have a far better chance of being asked to speak at another event, increase your sales, or close a multitude of other business deals.

Here's an example of how I talked about data without doing a data dump. I was giving a class on basic computer skills. For months I had been teaching different classes on how to use the mouse. I was getting bored with it. Class after class, different students of course, I would repeat the same material over and over. I would show them how to hold the mouse, how to scroll up and down, how to right click and left click. Eventually, I clued in that nobody was listening because I wasn't interesting. I decided to tell a story. A nurse I had been teaching thought she had to keep moving the mouse when she ran out of room on her desk. She literally ran it up the side of her monitor and across the top. Once I told that story, and once they had stopped laughing, everybody quickly figured out how to move the mouse properly.

I'm going to pick on architects for a moment. I recall attending a presentation by a large architectural firm. The presenter just dumped measurements, sizes, angles, on and on it went. He spoke as if someone had just died. I looked around the room and noticed that everyone was fighting sleep. No amount of coffee could save his presentation. He asked me afterwards what I thought. Here's the advice I gave him. Tell us the benefits of the building. Don't tell us that we'll have eight energy efficient bulbs per office. Tell us, with lots of enthusiasm, that the bulbs will keep our energy up all day, increasing our productivity and our mood. Better mood, better moral, better staff, better service...everybody wins. I suggested he tell us stories about past clients who followed his advice and what the benefits were. He immediately came up with three stories that were really funny. Problem solved. Great speaker plus great stories equals happier clients.

Chapter 8

Speaking with Notes

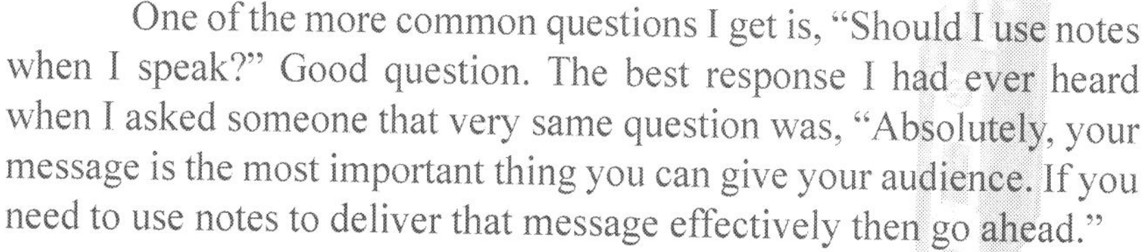

One of the more common questions I get is, "Should I use notes when I speak?" Good question. The best response I had ever heard when I asked someone that very same question was, "Absolutely, your message is the most important thing you can give your audience. If you need to use notes to deliver that message effectively then go ahead."

I would encourage you to review your speech before the presentation as much as time allows and then bring your notes with you to the presentation. The key to using notes is to not read from them during your speech. Use them only as a resource should you lose your train of thought. There is absolutely nothing wrong with finishing your sentence, moving to your notes, taking five seconds, finding your spot and going on with your next point.

Earlier I mentioned you want to know what direction your speech is going. If you know where your speech is going there will be little use for notes. You'll know your main points and what stories you want to use to cover those points. With some rehearsal exact words and sentence structure will come naturally.

If you still want to bring notes to the podium consider using one sheet of paper with only a few key words on it. Here is what my one sheet looks like:

1) Early Life
2) School
3) First Jobs
4) First Speech
5) Joining Toastmasters
6) Competing at the World Championships
7) Life after Losing
8) Creating new opportunities

Those few notes help keep me focused and remind me of the direction I want the speech to go in. I use a large bold font so I don't have to search for keys words. If I need a reminder during the speech, I walk by the podium and quickly glance towards the sheet of paper without anybody noticing. If I'm trying new material I'll tape my notes to the floor of the stage and glance downwards at them while speaking. There's an insider's secret if you've ever heard one.

Chapter 9

Body Language

The greatest difference between a good speaker and a GREAT speaker is that a great speaker moves with purpose. The best way to move with purpose is to develop a scene on your stage. What is the scene? Well, it's your living room…it's outdoors…it's wherever the story you are telling is set.

Example: When telling the story about my father's passing, I set the scene on the right side of the stage. I'll be very specific about the objects within the scene. I'll point to and describe the bed in one certain area, the medical equipment next to the bed and the chair at the foot of the bed. I'll never walk through the bed, the medical equipment or the chair. Not thrashing through your scene is critical. If you place an important object in your scene, it has to stay there visually for your audience, even though it's not really there. You generally won't have props on the stage but if you set the scene correctly the audience sees the props in their minds.

When telling a new story, walk to another part of the stage and set a new scene in a new area. Separate the two scenes. It wouldn't make sense for them to overlap and be in the same place. For instance, when telling a story about something that happened with my dad and me when I was young, I walk to the left of the stage and describe a local park. Then, later on in the speech, I tell a story about when my dad and I were older and fishing. I set my new scene for my new story in a new area on the stage. I walk across the stage with PURPOSE to make a new and different point.

Center Stage

My personal preference is to leave center stage for very dramatic events. I use it for the beginning of my speech, the end of my speech and my big points. I face the audience straight on, shoulders square and make sure I make eye contact with someone when I deliver the big lines.

When do I move?

This can be answered with the section above. You move in between, around your scenes, but never through your scenes. You move when describing something you tasted, smelled, heard or felt. You use your hands to accentuate what you are describing. You have to be careful not to look over rehearsed. I saw a speaker touch her heart every time she mentioned how sad or emotional she felt about a particular event in her life. It looked overly rehearsed. In real life situations you wouldn't touch your heart every time you told someone you were sad. You might shake your head, look away, or you may even put your hands through your hair. You have many options to use when describing events and using body language.

You will often hear speakers tell other speakers to "be natural". The reality is that books like this one are written because "be natural" simply isn't that easy. The only way it will become natural is to work up the courage and speak as often as you can. How would you move if you were telling a story at a family event? Whatever would be natural in those situations would look natural on stage. The only difference is that your movements should be larger when you're on stage.

Small Movements

Try to keep your movements simple at first. If you speak often your motions will become larger and more frequent. If your only goal is to give some toasts or introduce someone at an event, keep it simple. You don't have to feel the need to move that much at all. All you're doing is saying, "Please welcome Mr. Ralph Jones to the stage." No great movement required there. The next time you can try, "Please give a huge hand of applause for your President, Mrs. Helen Smith." Perhaps the only movement you'll do here is clap your hands to get the audience engaged. Now your confidence is growing. How about trying, "I truly love and respect this next speaker. I'd like to ask everyone to please stand and welcome Mr. Tom Robertson." Again, no great movement here, but you might have paused after saying, "I truly love and respect this next speaker." A pause is a very powerful tool. It forces the audience to lean in and listen to what is about to be said next. It shows tremendous confidence.

Recently I saw a very gifted speaker talk about the many nights he went to bed hungry while growing up in Ghana, Africa. Instead of just saying, "I was so hungry. Night after night we went to bed starving." He said something like, "I was so hungry. Night after night I would imagine eating the most delicious foods, with all kinds of spices. Slowly my hunger would disappear as I licked the salt from my fingers." It was the coolest thing I'd ever seen a speaker do, he actually quickly licked some of his finger tips. Not a big gesture but a simple one that added tremendous visual effect.

Big Movements

As the Booya Speaker, I'm all about BIG MOVEMENTS. It wasn't always that way. I used to take up very little space on stage. I felt very aware of my body language, especially my hands. Over time, however, I learned to completely forget about my body and focus on the message. Once you focus on your message your body will react accordingly. Since my job is to inspire people I believe my stories should be high energy. How do you create energy? Through motion! I jump around on stage, I sing, I wave my hands everywhere, I do whatever it takes as long as my actions are congruent with the point I'm trying to make.

Focus on your message first and watch the body language come through. It's a process. Film yourself. As you watch yourself on video you will find spots where you can add body language or remove it. The more confident you become the more natural it will all become.

Where do I put my hands?

In the real world you generally don't think, "Hey, what should I do with my hands?" As a new speaker let your hands start at your side, then as your story moves ahead, let them do their own thing. Some people think it's a huge no-no to have your hands in your pockets. I disagree. In the real world we put our hands in our pockets all the time. I've seen many great speakers, Booya Speakers like Darren Lacroix, Ed Tate and Sherly Roush place their hands in their pockets. Again, as a new speaker your hands will start off in your pockets, but as you start talking they will come out and take on a life of their own. They will naturally start behaving as hands do, they will be natural and become part of the story. If, however, your hands remain in your pockets for your entire speech, that's a problem! Free them.

Chapter 10

I Want To Be A Speaker – Where Do I Begin?

This chapter is for those who would like to become full or part time professional speakers. There are so many questions people have once they decide they want to become a speaker. The overwhelming question is…. "How do I become a speaker?" Quickly followed by, "Where to I begin?" The next question usually is, "Should I ask to get paid or should I do it for free?"

The Beginning

Toastmasters International

The best place to start out as a speaker is to join Toastmasters International. It is hands down the number one, nonprofit organization in the world for communication and leadership skills development. You can go up there, FAIL and still receive applause. Nobody expects you to be perfect at Toastmasters. They just want you to try. You can begin by speaking in small roles until you feel comfortable. Slowly you can increase how often you speak and the length of your speeches. Many new members simply start by introducing themselves and that's all they do for a number of weeks. Many professional speakers got their start at Toastmasters.

During the first few months you'll learn how to hone your skills, tell a story and control the jitters. Once you feel comfortable, you can even compete in the World Championships of Public Speaking, Tall Tales, or Humorous Speech Contests. Most clubs meet once a week. I highly recommend it as a way to begin.

Be The One Who Speaks Up

It was long before joining Toastmasters I knew I would become a speaker. In fact, I can clearly remember giving my first speech. I was nine years old and attending a local hockey awards banquet. The emcee asked if any of the kids wanted to come up and tell a joke. I thought to myself, "Dad told a joke a few weeks ago that everybody thought was really funny. I'll tell that one." I went to the stage, grabbed the microphone and saw my mom and dad sitting in the front row looking so proud. I started telling the joke. My mom started shaking her head, "No, no, no." My dad, however, couldn't have been prouder. I told the most profane joke any nine year ever told and it completely leveled the room (leveling the room is a good thing). I was hooked on public speaking from that moment on.

You need to look for ways to become "that person." Look for opportunities at the dinner table, weddings, parties and family events to tell stories or give a speech. For example, my dad passed away in September 2010, he was very proud that I had become a speaker and entertainer. We would sit on his porch after supper and he would tell anyone who walked by, "Hey, this is my son, the entertainer and speaker." I decide that during dinner, after the funeral, I would do my very best to make sure everyone sitting at my table had a great evening, filled with stories and laughter. I told a bunch of stories that involved my father. I could hear him laughing and saying, "You got it Martin, keep it going." I can hear him laughing as I write this paragraph. He'd slap his knee as he laughed. I miss that.

Using every opportunity to tell a story or be in front of others helps build your confidence and hone your speaking skills. Speak up!

Take It To The Next Level

Join the local Chamber of Commerce in your area. They are always looking for people to speak at their luncheons or other events. Don't forget to look into speaking at the Women in Business lunches, even if you are a man. Don't limit yourself, there are speaking opportunities everywhere. Don't look for excuses not to go, just go and give them a reason to hire you. Meet and introduce yourself to as many people as possible and let them know you love to speak. Always introduce yourself as an expert in your field first and a speaker second. You are an expert who loves to speak!

Look for other clubs and associations in your area that you can join and attend their meetings on a regular basis. Then speak up and volunteer to speak!

Google "associations", "conferences" and "event planners" to find organizations looking for a speaker. While it may be exciting to know that some of these associations are actually willing to pay for a speaker, don't focus on that. Focus on your story and message. Concentrate on what message you want to convey, what conferences are a good match to bring that message to and see if you can speak at them. If they offer to pay you, great!! But focus on getting the experience in the beginning.

Remember, it will take some time. You may find that it takes two or three years to get where you want to be as a speaker in terms of your confidence and your ability to connect on a consistent basis, fortunately it's not a race. The idea is simply to become comfortable and confident enough to be able to bring your message to a group of five, fifty or even five hundred people.

Lastly, remember to take the time and money to invest in yourself. Go to one or two conferences a year to learn about the speaking industry. Research what conferences would make a wise investment for you. In 2010 I attended Author 101 in Las Vegas. My goal was to learn how to turn my passion for teaching presentation skills into a book in less than six months without going through a publisher. This book is the result.

Fees

At the beginning of your speaking career do not expect to be paid every time you speak. This is a time to hone your craft. I know there are speakers out there who will disagree with me on not asking for payment when you are just starting out. If someone offers to pay you, I'm not saying you have to turn down the opportunity to make some cash, go ahead, take the money. What I am saying, however, is if you are asked to speak at a local community event, a rotary club or high school grad ceremony I would recommend that you not turn them down simply because they don't have a budget to pay you. Eventually, once you've established yourself as an expert who speaks, you will have every right to say, "I have valuable information that has taken years to learn. It's only fair I be paid to share this knowledge."

Become an Expert First

In the previous paragraph I wrote, "Once you've established yourself as an expert who speaks." Establish yourself as an expert first and speaker second. Once I understood this notion I became much more marketable.

In March of 2010, while teaching a class on public speaking, I asked one of the students what he spoke about. His response was typical of many new speakers. It was a response I had used many times in the past. He said, "Martin, I can speak on anything. I just love to speak." I loved his enthusiasm but his approach needed some tweaking. Realistically when someone is looking to hire a speaker they do not hire someone just to speak. They want someone with experience, some expertise, or a level of knowledge that the audience doesn't have. The gentleman I was speaking with was in his 60's. He was full of great stories and experience. We sat down and uncovered his area of expertise and how to position himself as an expert first and speaker second. It completely changed the way he thought about creating speaking opportunities and how to market himself.

How Do You Position Yourself As An Expert?

The hardest period I ever went through as a speaker was when I realized I had to take a step backwards. I had been trying to speak for a couple of years and couldn't seem to book as many speeches as I wanted to. If I did book an event, three people showed up.

I hired a business coach and learned how to position myself as an expert first. She told me that once I had shown the industry, associations and event planners that I had done my homework I would get more speaking gigs. I took a full year away from trying to book speaking engagements and I worked on establishing the necessary infrastructure to establish myself as an expert and allow people to get to know me as a speaker. You may want to consider working on the following items to position yourself as an expert first and speaker second:

1.)	Hire a Web designer and establish a Web site on your expertise. Make sure that you have a section dedicated to your speaking. For an example, visit my Web site at www.Martin Presse.com. If you are a new speaker contact Cynthia Lay otherwise known as The Butterfly Herder. She only works with speakers. She understands their needs and will make sure you get a great Web site.

2.)	Start working on a book. Write about your area of expertise, whether that's sales, leadership or party planning, just write a book. If you want to learn how to write a book in thirty days google "Craig Duswalt, Rock Star System for Success." He has a formula for self publishing a book very quickly. Consider hiring a ghost writer. Your book may not sell a million copies but it will position you as an expert in your field. It gives you instant credibility with audiences, event planners and associations. Why? Because all else being equal, if they are considering two speakers for an event and you've written a book and the other speaker has not, you will be seen as the expert.

3.)   Post videos of your speeches on Youtube.com.

4.)   Write blogs on your own website or blogging websites.

5.)   Create audio CDs and DVDs.
   a.   Buy a Flip video recorder, a camcorder, and digital recorder.
   b.   Purchase a great microphone such as the ones used by radio stations and record directly from your pc. I own a Samson G Track mic. It looks like what Larry King used. I can be twelve feet away and it'll pick up my voice perfectly.

6.)   Write articles for local newspapers and trade magazines.

7.)   Use social networking to your advantage. Setup accounts on Facebook, Twitter and LinkedIn. Learn how to use those accounts to build a fan base.

8.)   Attend seminars. Once people see you often enough they will assume you are serious about becoming a speaker. I was given this advice, "Martin, it's not who you know, it's who knows you." Now that I've attended a few seminars it's amazing who I can call if I have any questions.

   Once you have positioned yourself as an expert who speaks the speaking gigs will slowly add up. How? One option is to start making phone calls. Call companies and organizations that could benefit from your expertise. Volunteer to speak at their meetings and conferences.

You could also put on a seminar of your own. This can be costly and with little financial reward initially but over time people will talk and start attending your seminars. You'll also learn a great deal about marketing, sales and customer relations while putting on your seminars. I've found them to be a terrific learning tool. If you've joined Toastmasters and other associations let people know you are ready to start speaking. I wouldn't recommend you quit your job just yet, but I do believe that slowly and surely you will be asked to speak more often as you build a presence.

Chapter 11

Quick Tips – Your Reference Guide

1.)   <u>Tell your Story</u>

Focus on telling YOUR story. Tell us your Firsts, Fears, Frustrations and Failures. Use anecdotes, analogies, activities and acronyms to deliver powerful messages. Get to the conflict quickly and then let the tension rise. Take yourself off the pedestal. Tell us what you learned and the benefits of the lesson.

2.)   <u>Only Tell Small Bits of Other Peoples' Stories</u>

Other peoples' stories are only used to enhance or back up your own story. They shouldn't be the primary experience you want the audience to focus on. The audience is there to learn from you and about you. They want to listen to what happened to you. They want to learn from your experiences. I hear so many speakers talk about Dr. Martin Luther King, John F. Kennedy and Mother Theresa. They undoubtedly lived incredible lives, filled with passion and purpose but too often they dominate the speakers speech. Use them only as brief examples and focus on the experiences you've had. I recall coming to the end of a speech at one time, I asked if anyone had any questions about the material I had covered. Guess what happened, they only asked questions about what happened in my life regarding the topic I had covered. In this case I was speaking about the entertainment industry but I had talked a great deal about other entertainers and their experiences.

Lesson learned, talk about your experience and make it relevant to your audience.

3.) <u>Use PowerPoint Sparingly</u>

Go out and take a PowerPoint course. Then forget about it. Initially I leaned on PowerPoint too much. An attendee finally spoke up and said, "Martin, you are the speaker. You are the presentation. They have come to see you speak, not the charts and graphs and 50-60 pages of text on a PowerPoint presentation." Today I rarely use PowerPoint slides. I might use four or five slides for a ninety minute speech. I gave an eight hour session on public speaking in 2009 and used no slides to prove a point; you can give powerful presentations without PowerPoint.

4.) <u>Open with a BIG BANG</u>

No more "Thank you on Mrs. Johnson for having me, I really appreciate the opportunity." No more airport stories. We've all heard them and the audience will stop listening to you. Open with a big bang as soon as you hit the stage. As soon as you are introduced…pause… then – DO SOMETHING DIFFERENT. Here's a list of options:

a.) Ask a question. Some may require an action
- Raise Your Hand if You've Ever Been In Love.
- Would $1,000,000.00 make you happy. Are you sure?
- Do you trust your staff? Do you think they steal from you?

b.) Make a Bold Statement
- I do not believe that more people are afraid of dying than making a speech.
- In America today, over 75% of the population read less than three non fiction books in their lives once they finish high school.

- There are six key action steps you must take if you're going to be a leader.

c.) **Make a Big Promise**
- By the end of this speech you will know the four ways to create fabulous speeches.
- In the next sixty minutes you will understand six ways to get any customer to buy your product.
- You can make a six figure income using the internet.

Generally the audience won't be expecting you to say any of these things as you open your speech. Notice how they'll lean in wondering what you'll say next.

5.) <u>The "You" Versus "I' Rule</u>

When you video and audio tape yourself pay attention to how many times you say "I" versus "you." Change your "I" into "You" as much as possible. For instance, instead of talking about my bankruptcy and making it all about "me" and "I", I changed as much as I could to, "you may know how that feels. Have you ever had creditors calling you day and night?" and so forth. I started doing that a few years ago and noticed an immediate impact with my audience. Try it and see how it works for you.

6.) <u>Never End with a Q&A</u>

Signal to the audience that you are about to end. Say something like, "I'm going to take about five minutes for some Q&A and then we'll wrap it up." That lets people know not to leave right after the last question. You still have something of value to say after the Q&A.

I have heard POWERFUL speeches where the speaker ended with, "Okay, let's have some questions" only to be followed by awkward SILENCE. That is not a powerful way to end a speech. If you want to have some Q&A start with one of your own or plan ahead and ask someone to ask you a question during the Q&A.

Most importantly end the speech with a story that wraps everything up and makes a powerful point. Send them home filled with hope, not a weak Q&A that fizzles.

7.)   <u>Take Yourself Off the Pedestal</u>

Time and time again I hear speakers who make themselves the hero of the story. They were the cause of change, they were the hero or the one who taught everyone a powerful lesson. This strategy will make you unrelatable. You want to be the one who LEARNED the lesson. You don't want to be "special." If the audience sees you as being special they won't connect with you. A lot of them will think "He's special, unique, I'm nothing like that." Instead, talk about your flaws, what you had to overcome and sell the benefits behind the lesson you learned.

8.)   <u>Encourage Audience Participation</u>

Consider doing this soon after you begin speaking, preferably within the first three to five minutes of your speech. Ask them questions. Have them raise their hand if X has ever happened to them. Ask yes or no questions. Have them nod if they agree or disagree.

9.)   <u>Be Specific</u>

Be very specific when you are getting your point across. The beauty is in the details. For example, I changed, "I went bankrupt several years ago" to "In 1998 I went bankrupt and lost my family because of it." Stay away from sentences like, "There were a few people." Instead consider using, "There were eight people in the room during my first speech." Be specific in every sense. How heavy was it? How bright? What did it smell like, taste like? Give exact dates and timelines. All these things will make your story come to life and get your point across with perfect clarity.

10.) <u>Invite the Audience into Your Scene</u>

One of your goals is to have the audience be part of the event that changed your life. Practice statements like, "If you had been with me..", "If you had seen" or "If you had felt the cold water splash over me for three hours you too would have felt the slow painful onset of hypothermia." The last example is a meant to demonstrate the importance of being specific. Start by inviting the audience in, then get specific, set the emotional tone and bring the audience all the way into the scene by asking them how they would have felt, how they would have reacted, what they would have done or thought? This is referred to as the Tap and Transport method. You tap into their world by asking a question and transport them into your world by inviting them in. Here's an example of the Tap and Transport Method from beginning to end:

"Have you ever been stuck in the middle of a raging river, wondering if you might be swept way to your death ? (That's the TAP). In 2001 I found myself in such a situation. If you had been sitting with me on a cold boulder no bigger than your kitchen table what do you think would have gone through your mind" ? (We've now Transported them next to you on the boulder).

11.) <u>Match the Audience's Energy Level</u>

On occasion I've seen speakers go on stage and give over the top openings when the audience wasn't quite ready for it. Booya Speakers try to feel the energy in the room first. You may be excited to speak but fight the desire to bound up on stage saying, "WOW!!!! Can you FEEL the energy in this room?!?!? It's AWESOME!!!!" Not realizing the last speaker had the audience in tears, leaving the room in a bit of an emotional downer. By the way never do this. Always leave your audience uplifted. Always leave the audience inspired and filled with hope.

Pay attention to the audience's energy level and match it, then bring it to the level you want it to be.

12.)   <u>Use the Pause to Your Advantage</u>

Learn to love the silence! When you make a powerful point, pause and let it sink in. Take a few steps during your pause, plant your feet solidly and then start your next message. The worst thing a speaker can do after making a powerful point is to keep talking. The message completely loses its power and meaning. Get comfortable with the silence and pause.

13.)   <u>Scan Your Audience</u>

Years ago I had two bad habits when speaking to an audience. I would either look at the ground or look at the back of the room. Rarely would I look at anyone in the eye. The most powerful thing you can do when speaking is to look people in the eye, either one on one or when addressing an audience. Find one or two people in the audience and hold their gaze for one or two seconds after making an important point. Move on, scan and find someone else, pause, hold their gaze and scan again. Remember to, "Speak to one but look to many." This is where scanning comes in handy. I like to make my point, catch someone's eye and then move on to look at everyone in the room.

14.)   <u>Use the 4F's to Find Fabulous Stories</u>

When trying to find the very best stories to share with audiences talk about your Firsts, Fears, Frustrations and Failures. Using those circumstances will automatically take you off the perceived pedestal and give you the appearance of being "the same" as anybody in the audience.

Chapter 12

Parting Thoughts

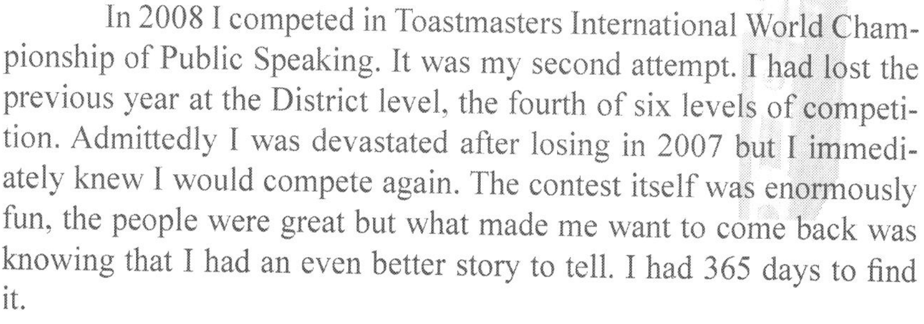

In 2008 I competed in Toastmasters International World Championship of Public Speaking. It was my second attempt. I had lost the previous year at the District level, the fourth of six levels of competition. Admittedly I was devastated after losing in 2007 but I immediately knew I would compete again. The contest itself was enormously fun, the people were great but what made me want to come back was knowing that I had an even better story to tell. I had 365 days to find it.

After the 2007 contest I bought a book called "The Nuts and Bolts of Public Speaking" by Craig Valentine. I flew to Mexico in February of 2008 before the contest season began and read the book while sipping margaritas. The book changed the way I looked at public speaking. I had been entirely too focused on myself when speaking. I was "in my head" much of the time, acting instead of reacting. If you pick up a book or take a class on acting you'll learn that acting is all about reacting.

I flew to Baltimore in March of 2008 to meet with Craig and get his advice on a speech I had written. We sat in his living room for two days. I can tell you without hesitation those were the hardest two days of my life. I had a migraine 4 hours into the first day. It didn't leave until I left for the airport the following day. Craig had me focus on and question everything I did on stage. Why did I stand a certain way, why did I say a certain word this way or that way? And pausing...more pausing. Craig noticed that I had read his book and had implemented many of the techniques he mentioned. I believe Craig had me question much of what I was doing so I would reflect carefully on how to have maximum impact.

After leaving Craig's place I felt equipped to create and deliver a much better speech. Leaving Craig's place, however, was just the beginning. Now I had to fly on my own.

I did well during the 2008 contest season. I won the club, area, and division contests feeling quite comfortable. The first big test was the District contest. In my case it encompassed the nine best speakers from Alberta and Saskatchewan (Canada). I managed to win using the speech Craig had coached me on. The message was about committing to your swing (your dreams and vision). According to the rules I was now required to write a whole new speech for the upcoming Regional contest, no more than seven and a half minutes in length, about seven hundred words.

I flew to Rapid City, South Dakota in June and competed in the Regional contest with a speech I really liked. It was about the power of words. As simple as they may be, some words can have a tremendous impact. I focused on one sentence, "I believe in you." During the speech I could hear gasps from the audience as I relived a particularly tender moment between my son and I. I finally knew what it meant to be "in the moment." I really didn't care if I won or lost that day. I gave the speech I had envisioned myself giving, with all the purpose, passion and commitment I could muster. The other speakers did a fine job and I knew they would make our region proud during the Finals. But I won...off to the Finals I would go.

Typically the Finals are in some beautiful, exotic, warm location. I earned my spot in the Finals and guess where I would get to go... Calgary, Canada. I like Calgary but I like Vegas even more.

I was again required to write a brand new speech. That made three speeches in eight months. No easy feat. It requires a fair amount of soul searching to write a speech that has depth, humor and flow. I worked very hard during those final eight weeks but I had simply run out of ideas. With the speaking experience I had at the time I simply couldn't find a story or message that touched me. If the message doesn't touch you, it probably won't touch the audience either.

I finally decided on a story about a young man whom I had taught to read. The message wasn't very clear. It was something along the lines of ,"Sometimes you just have to say No More." The young man had grown sick and tired of being a "have not" and when he said, "No more" he learned to read. It's a good story. I've used it in several speeches and audiences have always reacted favorably. I should have used it but I didn't.

Three days before the contest I decided to write a brand new speech. Essentially I choked. The pressure of doing well totally got to me. I lost my focus and made a decision that ultimately took me out of contention. I wrote a new speech in less than seventy-two hours, stayed up the entire night prior to the contest trying to memorize the speech, the logic and the flow. It was awful. The event started at 9a.m., August 16. I arrived at the convention center and saw the largest audience I had ever spoken in front of: twenty-five hundred people. All the work I had done the previous three days left me. I went back stage to relax and go over the speech again. I couldn't remember the first three lines. Nothing. Memories of being the emcee at the small town country music festival came flooding back. I suddenly found myself in a bathroom stall unable to move. "Martin, just the first three lines" I thought to myself...blank. I decided to go back into the hall and tell the chairman I wanted to pull out of the contest. I met up with a few friends on the way back in. Thumbs up from everyone, big smiles and lots of words of encouragement.

As I walked to the stage to find the chairman I ran into a contestant who'd been to the finals three times. A fellow by the name of JA Gamache. JA is a French speaking Canadian from Montreal. I too am from a small town just outside of Montreal and speak French. I introduced myself and told him how nervous I was. We connected immediately. I introduced him to my kids. JA has a big smile, warm eyes and an energy that fills the largest rooms. If anyone would understand how I felt it would be JA and he came through big time. He put the whole speaking thing into perspective just when I needed it most. He asked me a few questions to put me at ease.

"Martin you speak English right?"

I laughed, "Yeah, I do."

"Good, so language won't be a problem. You won't have to worry about that. What about a story Martin, do you have a story you want to share?"

"Yes...but I can't remember what I want to say."

This is where JA went deep. "Forget about what you want to say. Forget about the words, forget about where you want to stand and forget about the judges. You aren't here for that. You know the story, you lived it. You've probably told the story to your friends many times. Tell us the story and get off the stage." JA was on a roll now. "Look at this room, it's huge...so be big, be huge. Talk only to the people at the back of the room. Forget about everyone else, reach out to those people. One person needs to hear your message Martin, find that person, tell that person your story...they need to hear it."

That was all I needed to hear. On that particular day I knew exactly who needed to hear it. Patti, Kali and Alex. My lifeline. Patti is my ex, oddly enough she's also one of my closest friends. Without her I'm not sure what I would have become. Kali and Alex are her kids from a previous marriage. They are the reason I get up in the morning and why I have achieved many of the goals I've set for myself so far in this world. My speech was about them and how they showed me what it means to have a heart, to give unselfishly and to live with passion, purpose and commitment.

I may not have won that day but the lesson wasn't lost. I was asked recently what it really means to be a Booya Speaker. In one short sentence: Booya Speakers speak from the heart, they speak with passion, purpose and commitment. If you do those four things the audience will be in the palm of your hands.

Booya!

For more information on
Martin Presse's presentations, seminars,
keynotes, books and audio/dvd products
please call 780 361-0414 or
email martin@martinpresse.com

Please visit www.martinpresse.com

Made in the USA
Charleston, SC
06 September 2013